THE GOLF
QUOTATION BOOK

The Golf Quotation Book

A Clubhouse Companion

Edited by

MICHAEL HOBBS

ROBERT HALE · LONDON

Preface and selection © Michael Hobbs 1992
First published in Great Britain 1992

ISBN 0 7090 4424 0

Robert Hale Limited
Clerkenwell House
Clerkenwell Green
London EC1R 0HT

Photoset in Goudy by
Derek Doyle & Associates, Mold, Clwyd.
Printed in Hong Kong

Preface

I t is the relatively slow-moving games and sports which produce the best writing. Writers seem able to convey the flavour of, say, association football, rugby, or hockey, but to be less well able to describe in detail the various moments of truth. These flash upon the retina and, more often than not, are gone.

Cricket and golf are amongst the most slow-moving games and have attracted the talents of many excellent writers. Not that golf is slow in its entirety. I cannot, for instance, think of another sport where the striking implement is swung as fast while the object struck whisks away at a much higher muzzle velocity still.

But for the rest, it is undeniably a game played at slow speed – yet very high tension. The tension comes mainly because it is not a reaction sport. You may have an opponent – or perhaps 200 or more opponents in strokeplay competitions at various competitive levels – but, except psychologically, they should have no effect on the individual golfer. He has two main tasks.

One is to strike the ball at exactly the right speed. This applies equally to the full drive and the short putt. In each case, the margin for error is often slim indeed. For a long shot, just a few degrees of directional error mean the difference between a perfect shot and being buried in gorse, under water, or out of bounds. Pace of swing can often be just as significant. A shot honing in on the flag may be directionally exact but this is no good at all if the ball comes to rest many yards short or long.

The other task is to think your way through the problems set by the particular golf course. The player must make decisions which should be neither over-bold nor, on the other hand, too timorous.

Most of the time, such problems become one. The player must simply master himself.

However, most of the situations which occur in golf have parallels of a sort in other sports. For instance, missing a very short putt in golf is not so different from failing with an easy pot in snooker or missing a short kick from in front of the posts in rugby.

Where golf is truly different, however, is where it is played. A field, ground or stadium may be thought the centrepiece of its sport, like Lord's, Wimbledon, The Arms Park, Old Trafford, Hurlingham ... May I suggest that none of these excels a golf course in visual appeal, even one built on cold clay soil on a drear mid-winter's day?

Golf has been fortunate in its writers. One of the great essayists, Bernard Darwin, devoted much of his life to the game, while in recent years my own favourites have mainly been American.

The wittiest man who ever wrote about golf was Sir Walter Simpson, towards the end of the last century, while a near contemporary, Horace Hutchinson, was not far behind.

Even so, I suspect my own favourite remarks are those from the fifteenth century, drafted by clerks to the kings of Scotland, which berated the game, successively decreeing that it be 'utterly cryed downe', 'abused in time cumming', and declaring that it was an 'unproffitable sporte'.

True enough, if you wanted the citizenry to practise their archery and spearsmanship to be better able to confront the hated English. In less warlike times, golf – in part through its suitability for a handicap system which really works – to me, has shown itself to be the sport which best suits both the athlete at peak performance level and the man whose great weekly exertion is to pick up his Sunday newspaper with its supplements.

MICHAEL HOBBS

It is decreeted and ordained, that the Weapon-shawinges be halden be the Lordes and Baronnes Spiritual and Temporal, four times in the zeir. And that the Fute-ball and Golfe be utterly cryed downe, and not to be used. And as tuitching the Fute-ball and the Golfe, to be punished by the Barronniss un-law.

JAMES II OF SCOTLAND, 1457

Fute-ball and Golfe be abused in time cumming, and that the buttes be made up, and schuting used.

JAMES III OF SCOTLAND, 1471

The Honourable Company of Edinburgh Golfers parade the Silver Club in 1744.

9

It is statute and ordained that in na place of the Realme there be used Fute-ball, Golfe, or uther sik unproffitable sportes.

JAMES IV OF SCOTLAND, 1491

John Gardiner, James Bowman, Laurence Chalmers, and Laurence Cuthbert confess that they were playing at the golf on the North Inch in time of preaching after noon on the Sabbath. The Session rebuked them, and admonished them to resort to the hearing of the Word diligently on the Sabbath in time coming, which they promised to do.

KIRK SESSION OF PERTH, 1599

I was shown one particular set of golfers, the youngest of whom was turned of four-score. They were all gentlemen of independent fortunes who had amused themselves with this pastime for the best part of a century without ever having felt the least alarm from sickness or disgust; and they never went to bed without having each the best part of a gallon of claret in his belly. Such uninterrupted exercise, co-operating with the keen air from the sea, must, without all doubt, keep the appetite always on edge, and steel the constitution against all the common attacks of distemper.

TOBIAS SMOLLETT
The Expedition of Humphrey Clinker

What earthly good is golf? Life is stern and life is earnest. We live in a practical age. All around us we see foreign competition making itself unpleasant. And we spend our time playing golf! What do we get out of it? Is golf any *use*? That's what I'm asking you. Can you name me a single case where devotion to this pestilential pastime has done a man any practical good?

> P.G. WODEHOUSE
> *The Clicking of Cuthbert*

On the golf course, a man may be the dogged victim of inexorable fate, be struck down by an appalling stroke of tragedy, become the hero of unbelievable melodrama, or the clown in a side-splitting comedy.

> ROBERT TYRE JONES
> *The World of Golf*

Golf is more exacting than racing, cards, speculation or matrimony. In almost all other games you pit yourself against a mortal foe; in golf it is yourself against the world: no human being stays your progress as you drive your ball over the face of the globe.

> ARNOLD HAULTAIN
> *The Mystery of Golf*

There is no shape nor size of body, no awkwardness nor ungainliness, which puts good golf beyond reach. There are good golfers with spectacles, with one eye, with one leg, even with one arm. In golf, while there is life there is hope.

> SIR WALTER SIMPSON
> *The Art of Golf*

When I look on my life and try to decide out of what I have got most actual pleasure, I have no doubt at all in saying that I have got more out of golf than anything else.

> LORD BRABAZON
> *The Brabazon Story*

A tolerable day, a tolerable green, a tolerable opponent, supply, or ought to supply, all that any reasonably constituted human being should require in the way of entertainment. With a fine sea view, and a clear course in front of him, the golfer should find no difficulty in dismissing all worries from his mind, and regarding golf, even it may be indifferent golf, as the true and adequate end of man's existence. No inconvenient reminiscences of the ordinary workaday world, no intervals of weariness or monotony interrupt the pleasures of the game.

> EARL BALFOUR
> *Golf*

Golf is a game to teach you about the messages from within, about the subtle voices of the body-mind. And once you understand them you can more clearly see your 'hamartia', the ways in which your approach to the game reflects your entire life. Nowhere does a man go so naked.

> MICHAEL MURPHY
> *Golf in the Kingdom*

Golf has drawbacks. It is possible, by too much of it, to destroy the mind.

> SIR WALTER SIMPSON
> *The Art of Golf*

The humour of golf is a divine comedy in the deepest sense. Like all sources of laughter it lies in contrast and paradox; in the thought of otherwise grave men gravely devoting hours and money to a technique which so often they, apparently alone, do not know they can never master. The solemnity of their eternal failure is vastly comic. The perpetualness of their hope is nobly humorous.

> R.C. ROBERTSON-GLASGOW

Excessive golfing dwarfs the intellect. Nor is this to be wondered at when we consider that the more fatuously vacant the mind is, the better for play. It has been observed that absolute idiots play the steadiest.

SIR WALTER SIMPSON
The Art of Golf

In so many English sports, something flying or running has to be killed or injured; golf calls for no drop of blood from any living creature.

HENRY LEACH

Early Flemish Golfers

When that pre-historic Dutchman – or was he a Dane? – carried his kolb or club over to Leith in a smack, deep-laden with ankers of Schiedam, he little dreamt that he was draining the life-blood of his land and sprinkling its life-giving drops over the links of North Britain. The wildest dreams never forecast the numbers or the prowess of the stalwart men and lissome girls who now honour that Dutchman's memory and drive the wild eccentric guttie afar over the shining reaches by the sea.

W.F. COLLIER, 1890

The soldier, having sought the bubble reputation in the cannon's mouth, may earn laurels on a field which shall be bloodless and receive at least a purer pleasure from deftly landing his ball in the hole than ever came to him from letting daylight into his fellow mortals.

DR PROUDFOOT, 1890

Romeyn de Hooghe, Haarlem, c. 1650

However unlucky you may be, it really is not fair to expect your adversary's grief for your undeserved misfortunes to be as poignant as your own.

HORACE HUTCHINSON
Hints on Golf

A noble golfer was crossing the ferry in order to keep a tryst at Portrush. He had his clubs beside him. There they lay shapely, the object of much wonder to a gaping passenger. At last wonder grew into speech, 'Sorr, what's them quare things for?'

The golfer delivered an instructive lecture on the joys and sorrows of the game, to which the enquirer listened with quizzical eye – and finally remarked, 'What a quare lot o' ways of wasting time there is nowadays.'

W.F. COLLIER, 1890

If, then, happy men ought to play golf, what of miserable men? Let them also become golfers. 'What!' the reader exclaims, 'shall a man in misery take to golf?' Yes, most assuredly! In vain will a player with a woebegone countenance endeavour to go a round. Before he has played a couple of holes, he will brighten up, his whole aspect will become changed and happiness will shine forth on his face. And why so? Largely from that absorption in the events of the moment which the game demands. That miserable introspection from which such wretchedness springs is impossible in the golfer.

DR PROUDFOOT, 1890

Golf should be essentially a game of good fellowship; it should, and generally does, constitute a bond of union between any strangers who casually meet. But to welcome *some* who are seen on the links, to make them free of the guild, would require a larger reserve of brotherly love than can be laid claim to by the mass of golfing humanity.

H.S.C. EVERARD, 1890

16

The glorious thing is that thousands of golfers, in park land, on windy downs, in gorse, in heather, by the many-sounding sea, enjoy their imbecilities, revel in their infirmities, and from failure itself draw that final victory – the triumph of hope.

    R.C. ROBERTSON-GLASGOW

Golf is in the interest of good health and good manners. It promotes self-restraint and affords a chance to play the man and act the gentleman.

    PRESIDENT TAFT

Shall the married man play golf? This admits of no argument. Certainly. Of all the plagues to a woman in the house is a man during the day.

    DR PROUDFOOT, 1890

Golf is to me what his Sabine farm was to the poet Horace –
a solace and an inspiration.
    RAMSAY MACDONALD

Golf is the only game where the worst player gets the best of
it. He obtains more out of it as regards both exercise and
enjoyment, for the good player gets worried over the
slightest mistake, whereas the poor player makes too many
mistakes to worry over them.
    DAVID LLOYD GEORGE

It is a test of temper, a trial of honour, a revealer of character. It means going into God's out of doors, getting close to nature, fresh air and exercise, a sweeping of mental cobwebs and a genuine relaxation of tired tissues.

DAVID FORGAN

The poetic temperament is the worst for golf. It dreams of brilliant drives, iron shots laid dead, and long putts holed, while in real golf success waits for him who takes care of the foozles and leaves the fine shots to take care of themselves.

SIR WALTER SIMPSON
The Art of Golf

There is one man who ought never to appear on a golfing green. And this is the good man. Let him remain away. That immaculate creature whose life is spent in seeing his neighbour's faults and comparing them with his own wonderful perfection, is quite out of place among golfers. They are all men, not saints. Therefore let the Pharisee, whose pretentions to superiority we will not even dispute, keep at home.

DR PROUDFOOT, 1890

Golf is a science, the study of a lifetime, in which you can exhaust yourself but never your subject.

DAVID FORGAN

Unlike the other Scotch game of whisky drinking, excess in it is not injurious to the health.

SIR WALTER SIMPSON

Beyond the fact that it is a limitless arena for the full play of human nature, there is no sure accounting for golf's fascination. Obviously yet mysteriously, it furnishes its devotees with an intense, many-sided, and abiding pleasure unlike that which any other form of recreation affords. Perhaps it is, as Andrew Carnegie once claimed, an 'indispensable adjunct of high civilization'. Perhaps it is nothing more than the best game man has ever devised.

HERBERT WARREN WIND
The Complete Golfer

Caddie: Professor, you may have the degrees but you've got to have a head to play golf.

ANON.

Try to remember that a person may be a most indifferent golfer, and yet be a good Christian gentleman, and in some respects worthy of your esteem.

HORACE HUTCHINSON
Hints on Golf

Boy, if the phone should ring,
Or anyone come to call,
Whisper that this is spring,
To come again next fall.
Say I have a date on a certain tee
Where my friends the sand-traps wait in glee.

US GOLF CLUB SONG

I don't care to join any club that's prepared to have me as a member.

GROUCHO MARX

The least thing upset him on the links. He missed short putts because of the uproar of the butterflies in the adjoining meadows.

P.G. WODEHOUSE

A golfer needs a loving wife to whom he can describe the day's play through the long evenings.

P.G. WODEHOUSE

I guess there is nothing that will get your mind off everything like golf. I have never been depressed enough to take up the game but they say you get so sore at yourself you forget to hate your enemies.

WILL ROGERS

Golf is a game kings and presidents play when they get tired of running countries.

CHARLES PRICE

In golf, humiliations are the essence of the game.

ALISTAIR COOKE

Golf puts a man's character on the anvil and his richest qualities – patience, poise, restraint – to the flame.

BILLY CASPER

Golf is used by people of every colour, race, creed and temperament, in every climate. No recreation, apart from the simple contests of the river and field, has been so universal since the world began. There is no freemasonry like the freemasonry of golf. Our happy game has wound a bright cordon round the world and so does she play her part in the great evolution of general contentment.

HENRY LEACH

What golf has of honour, what it has of justice, of fair play, of good fellowship and sportsmanship – in a word, what is best in golf – is almost surely traceable to the inspiration of the Royal and Ancient.

    ISAAC GRAINGER

You get to know more of the character of a man in a round of golf than in six months of political experience.

    LLOYD GEORGE

Golf is typical capitalist lunacy.

    GEORGE BERNARD SHAW

Golf is a way of spoiling a good walk.

    MARK TWAIN

The quhilk day, David Gray pewdarer and Thomas Saith tailour being callit comperit, and, being accusit for prophaning of the Saboth day in playing at the gouf eftir nune, confest the samin; and becaus thai war nocht apprehendit with the lyik fault of befoir, thair war admonished nocht to do the samin heireftir.

ST ANDREWS KIRK SESSIONS, 1598

Golf is a game whose aim is to hit a very small ball into an even smaller hole, with weapons singularly ill-designed for the purpose.

SIR WINSTON CHURCHILL

The which day James Rodger, Johne Rodger, Andrew Howdan, and George Patersone, were complained upon for playing at the golf upon ane Lord's day; were ordained to be cited the next day. The which day compeired the aforementioned persons, and confessed thair profaining of the Lord's day by playing at the golf; were ordained to mak their publick repentance the next day.

The which day, Johne Howdan was deposed from his office, being ane deacon.

RECORDS OF THE KIRK SESSION OF HUMBIE, 1651

This all our life long we frolik and gay,
And instead of court revels, we merrily play,
At Trap, at Rules, and at Barley-break run,
At Goff and at Foot-Ball, and when we have done,
These innocent sports, we'll laugh and lie down.

THOMAS SHADWELL, 1671

My favourite shots are the practice swing and the conceded putt. The rest can never be mastered.

LORD ROBERTSON

Golf is life. If you can't take golf, you can't take life.
ANON.

The only way of really finding out a man's true character is to play golf with him. In no other walk of life does the cloven hoof so quickly display itself.
P.G. WODEHOUSE

Golfing excellence goes hand in hand with alcohol, as many an open and amateur champion has shown.
HENRY LONGHURST

I owe everything to golf. Where else would a guy with an IQ like mine make this much money?
HUBERT GREEN

Be funny on a golf course? Do I kid my best friend's mother about her heart condition?
PHIL SILVERS

If your adversary is badly bunkered, there is no rule against your standing over him and counting his strokes aloud, with increasing gusto as their number mounts up; but it will be a wise precaution to arm yourself with the niblick before doing so, so as to meet him on equal terms.
HORACE HUTCHINSON
Hints on Golf

A match at golf this day with Cozen Roger, and should have greatly beaten him but for what he said to me as we walked to the 15th tee, being by this time 2 upp. When he asks me: 'By the way, Sam, what is all this to do 'twixt you and your Mrs?' Which puts me in a pretty twitter as to what he has heard and what I shall best say to him, so that I did most vilely foozle my drive, and thereafter not a stroak could I strike clean.

SAMUEL PEPYS

It is a game in which the whole temperamental strength of one side is hurled against the strength of the other, and the two human natures are pressing bitterly and relentlessly against each other from the first moment of the game to the last. It is the whole man, mind and body. That is the meaning of the temperamental factor in golf, and that is why a great match at golf is great indeed.

HENRY LEACH

A tournament goes on for days. It is played at a dangerously high mental pressure. Golf makes its demands on the mind. A golfer is terribly exposed in almost every way. The responsibility is his and there is no way to camouflage this, no hope of jettisoning it.

PETER ALLISS
Alliss through the Looking Glass

When five up express, as is polite, regret at laying a stimy, but rejoice in your heart.

SIR WALTER SIMPSON
The Art of Golf

If you call on God to improve the results of a shot while it is still in motion, you are using 'an outside agency' and subject to appropriate penalties under the rules of golf.

HENRY LONGHURST

When the great snooker player Joe Davis saw his first game of golf the putting puzzled him. 'Why', he asked his golfing friend, 'don't they knock the ball into the hole first time?'

ANON.

That tremendous finish at Inverness hypnotized me. Think of it – five players having a chance to win, right up to the 72nd green. I concluded right there that the Open Championship was the thing. I confess it still is my idea of a tournament.

I watched Leo Diegel play the last three holes, and I remember wondering why his face was so grey and sort of fallen in. I found out for myself, later.

ROBERT TYRE JONES

If your adversary is a hole or two down, there is no serious cause for alarm in his complaining of a severely sprained wrist, or an acute pain, resembling lumbago, which checks his swing. Should he happen to win the next hole, these symptoms will in all probability become less troublesome.

    HORACE HUTCHINSON
    Hints on Golf

A perfectly unconscious style in a grown man is very rare. It will oftenest be found among professionals whose education does not tempt them to think. There is one illustrious and venerable champion of whom it is proverbial that not even a whole round of bad shots can tempt him to consider his position. 'I missed the ba',' is all he says. To hit it again is all he tries. It is wonderful how soon he succeeds.

    SIR WALTER SIMPSON
    The Art of Golf

Golfers are very fond of insisting, and with great justice, that the game is not won by the driver. It is the short game – the approaching and putting – that wins the match. Nevertheless, despite the truth of this, if there were no driving there would be very little golf.

    HORACE HUTCHINSON

There is the glorious sensation of making a true hit. This is not only true of the drive. There is a right or wrong way of hitting a yard putt. The right way is bliss, the wrong purgatory. The pleasure of the long drive or second shot to the green gives as fine an emotion as is possible for any sinner to receive on this earth.

    R.H. LYTTLETON

Hounsom Byles, 1895

The golfer is never old until he is decrepit. So long as providence allows him the use of two legs active enough to carry him round the green, and of two arms supple enough to take a 'half swing', there is no reason why his enjoyment in the game need be seriously diminished. Decay no doubt there is; long driving has gone for ever; and something less of firmness and accuracy may be noted even in the short game. But the decay has come by such slow gradations, it has delayed so long and spared so much, that it is robbed of half its bitterness.

> EARL BALFOUR
> *Golf*

Now golf is a game in which each player has a small hard ball of his own, which he strikes with a stick while it is quiescent, with the intention of putting it into a hole.

> SIR WALTER SIMPSON
> *The Art of Golf*

The game required a certain cold toughness of mind, and absorption of will. There was not an athlete I talked to from other sports who did not hold the professional golfer in complete awe, with thanksgiving that golf was not their profession .

> GEORGE PLIMPTON
> *The Bogey Man*

Golf is gaining so enormously in popularity, and so many now take an interest in the matches of good, and especially of professional players, that it would be a boon to a very large number of readers if reports of matches could be made more life-like, showing appreciation of the real turning points of the game and confining themselves less exclusively to a dry chronicling of details.

> HORACE HUTCHINSON, 1890

There is no such thing as a golfer uninterested in his driving. The really strong player seems to value his least; but this is merely because so many of his shots are good that they do not surprise him. Let it, however, be suggested that some other is a longer driver than he, and the mask of apathy will at once fall from his face, his tongue will be loosened, and he will proceed to boast.

> SIR WALTER SIMPSON

When the ball is down and the putter handed to the caddie, it is not well to say, 'I couldn't have missed it.' Silence is best. The pallid cheek and trembling lip belie such braggadocio.

> SIR WALTER SIMPSON
> *The Art of Golf*

You drive for show and putt for dough.

> ANON.

The best stroked putt in a lifetime does not bring the aesthetic satisfaction of a perfectly hit wood or iron shot. There is nothing to match the whoosh and soar, the almost magical flight of a beautifully hit drive or 5-iron.
AL BARKOW

A man who can putt is a match for anyone.
WILLIE PARK

While, on the whole, playing through the green is the part most trying to the temper, putting is that most trying to the nerves. There is always the hope that a bad drive may be redeemed by a fine approach shot, or that a 'foozle' with the brassy may be balanced by some brilliant performance with the iron. But when the stage of putting-out has been reached no further illusions are possible.
EARL BALFOUR
Golf

When a putter is waiting his turn to hole out a putt of one or two feet in length, on which the match hangs at the last hole, it is of vital importance that he think of nothing. At this supreme moment he ought to fill his mind with vacancy. He must not even allow himself the consolations of religion.

SIR WALTER SIMPSON
The Art of Golf

I took up golf as something to do when a wet pitch made cricket unplayable but soon I was playing when the sun shone as well. I gave it up soon after I married. I claimed it was a supreme sacrifice but the development of a cancerous slice probably had more to do with it.

People begin playing for so many reasons – exercise, because a friend plays, an injury has made some more physical game impossible, business contacts or often because the game is played in such beautiful surroundings.

We stop, sometimes, because of age. More often because we can't tolerate how badly we have come to play the game. The clubs come home and never go out again.

MICHAEL HOBBS
Golf for the Connoisseur

Walter Hay, goldsmith, accusit for playing at the boulis and golff upoun Sondaye in the tyme of the sermon.

RECORDS OF ELGIN, 1596

Long driving, if it be not the most deadly, is certainly the most dashing and fascinating part of the game; and of all others the principal difficulty of the Golfer to acquire, and his chief delight when he can manage it.

H.B. FARNIE, 1857

I forget when it happened but in the middle of a round, which I was regarding with the usual distaste, a small voice within me said: 'You don't *have* to do this,' and I thought, 'No, by God I don't.' A great wave of relief came over me and on D-Day, 1968, I put the clubs up in the loft with the water tanks, closed the hatch, removed the steps and walked away. Nor have I for one second regretted it. It was rather like having sucked a very good orange dry and realising you were eating the peel. Why not chuck it away and try an apple instead? Which is what I did.

> HENRY LONGHURST
> *My Life and Soft Times*

He struck Gysbert Cornelisz, tavern-keeper, and Claes Andriesz with a golf club at the house of Steven Jansz for which, together, he forfeits Fl. 20.

> COURT MINUTES OF THE COLONY OF RENSSE-
> LAERSWYCK, ALBANY, 1650

A good player who is a great putter is a match for any golfer. A great hitter who cannot putt is a match for no one.

> BEN SAYERS

Whoever plays ball with a club shall be fined 20 shillings or their upper garment.

> THE MAGISTRATES OF BRUSSELS, 1360

Golf is a better game played downhill.

> JACK NICKLAUS

The behaviour etiquette for greenside bunkers should go into reverse. Players should be forbidden to smooth them in any way. The bunker should be the fearful place it once was, not the perfect surface from which a pro expects to float his ball out stone dead, something he doesn't expect when chipping.

MICHAEL HOBBS

The next time you see a good player stalking backwards and forwards on the green, do not be led away by the idea that he is especially painstaking, but rather pity him for a nervous individual who is putting off the evil moment as long as he possibly can.

TED RAY

The person I fear most in the last two rounds is myself.

TOM WATSON

A good one iron shot is about as easy to come by as an understanding wife.

DAN JENKINS

We have these champions of the practice range who hit hundreds of shots but I think if you haven't got it when you get to a tournament you won't find it hitting away for hours. Use your brain, not your endurance.

PETER THOMSON

In America the Ryder Cup rates somewhere between the Tennessee Frog Jumping Contest and the Alabama Melon-Pip Spitting Championship, although the players themselves have always taken it seriously until Tom Weiskopf declined to play in favour of a week's holiday shooting sheep.

PETER DOBEREINER, 1978

The better you putt, the bolder you play.

DON JANUARY

Hitting a golf ball and putting have nothing in common. They're two different games. You work all your life to perfect a repeating swing that will get you to the greens, and then you have to try to do something that is totally unrelated. There shouldn't be any cups, just flag sticks. And then the man who hit the most fairways and greens and got closest to the pins would be the tournament winner.

BEN HOGAN

It may have been the greatest four-wood anyone ever hit. It was so much on the flag that I had to lean sideways to follow the flight of the ball.

GARY PLAYER

No one remembers who came second.

WALTER HAGEN

AVBREY
BEARDSLEY

I may go for it or I may not. It all depends on what I elect to do on my backswing.

BILLY JOE PATTON

Once the golfing champion allows himself to suspect that playing a superb round is not the be-all and end-all of life he is lost.

ANON.

James Waldie to have plaid att the golfe with the herds of Mulben; being found guilty they were rebuked for making so little conscience of the Lord's day, and ordained to make their publick repentance three Lord's days.

KIRK SESSIONS OF BOHARM, 1658

The ball people with their balls shall post themselves along the canal from the bridge in front of Master Arent Goes.

MAGISTRATES OF BERGEN OP ZOOM, 1461

Tennis is not in use amongst us, but in lieu of that, you have that excellent recreation of goff-ball than which truly I do not know a better.

THE MARQUIS OF ARGYLL, 1661

Nobody strikes the ball on the streets with clubs with lead or iron heads.

ORDINANCE OF ZIERIKZEE, 1429

Golf is the only game in which a precise knowledge of the rules can earn one a reputation for bad sportsmanship.

PATRICK CAMPBELL

Winners are a different breed of cat. They have an inner drive and are willing to give of themselves whatever it takes to win.

BYRON NELSON

Victory is everything. You can spend the money but you can never spend the memories.

KEN VENTURI

To be a champion, you have to find a way to get the ball in the cup on the last day.

TOM WATSON

I never pray on a golf course. Actually, the Lord answers my prayers everywhere except on the course.

BILLY GRAHAM

There is nothing to match the whoosh and the soar, the almost magical flight of a beautifully hit drive or five-iron. To go through all those movements of the body and get that result even once in a while is more thrilling than a hundred 10-foot putts that drop.

AL BARKOW

The more I practise, the luckier I get.

GARY PLAYER

A perfectly straight shot with a big club is a fluke.

JACK NICKLAUS

With the huge excited crowd surging all around him, it is only natural that the player should come in for a good deal of buffeting about. It may come as a surprise to many people to know after a big tournament my ankles and shins are black and blue.

HARRY VARDON

I feel calm in calm colours. I don't want people to watch the way I dress. I want people to watch the way I play.

SEVERIANO BALLESTEROS

The British Open probably would have died if the American stars hadn't started going over to play in it more regularly the last 15 years. Arnold Palmer saved it, but as far as I'm concerned he didn't do us any favours.

DAVE HILL

The hundred or so followers of the Royal and Ancient game who journeyed from Edinburgh on the morning of Thursday 22 September, the opening day, went prepared to have a thorough treat.

DAVID SCOTT DUNCAN
of the first Muirfield Open, 1892

Never break your putter and your driver in the same round or you're dead.

TOMMY BOLT

What an achievement it would be to set forth, properly and for all time, the glories of a golf tournament, the subtleties of mood, the severity of the strain, the infinite complexity and the pure simplicity that taken together make up the most stimulating sporting event of all.

MARK McCORMACK

What other people may find in poetry, I find in the flight of a good drive.
ARNOLD PALMER

Na inhabitants, be thameselffis, thair chiildren, servands, or fameleis, be sene at ony pastymes or gammis within or without the toun upoun the Sabbath day, sic as golf, aircherie, rowbowliss, penny stayne, katch pullis, or sic other pastymes.
EDICT OF EDINBURGH COUNCIL, 1592

The number one guys have to be almost totally self-centred. They have to possess an incredible burning for success. They have to ignore their friends and enemies and sometimes their families and concentrate entirely on winning. I couldn't survive that constant intensity, their ability to burn and burn and burn.
FRANK BEARD
Pro

The mark of a champion is the ability to make the most of good luck and the best of bad.
ANON.

His entire nature was bent on being a golfer. It is yet told on the links how Allan would rise betimes and, with shirt sleeves rolled up for better muscular play, start alone for practice across the deserted links, still wet with early dew. Allan has improved in his day on the old theories of golf and to him are owing many of the improved methods and styles of the present game.
Dundee Advertiser, 1859
of Allan Robertson

Mary Queen of Scots appears to have practised this game, for it was made a charge against her by her enemies, as an instance of her indifference to Darnley's fate, that she was seen playing at golf and pall-mall in the fields beside Seton a few days after his death.

Inventories of Mary Queen of Scots, 1863

Old Tom is the most remote point to which we can carry back our genealogical inquiries into the golfing style, so that we may virtually accept him as the common golfing ancestor who has stamped the features of his style most distinctly on his descendants.

HORACE HUTCHINSON, 1900
of Old Tom Morris

On being asked how good Young Tom Morris really was, an aged golfer replied: 'I cannot imagine anyone playing better.'

ANON.

Tommy Morris eclipsed his contemporaries and totally changed their conception of how well the game could be played – like Vardon, Jones and Hogan in later generations.
MICHAEL HOBBS

I went out to meet Johnny Ball and as he reeled off hole after hole in the right figure it became apparent that bar accidents he was going to do the most terrible thing that had ever yet been done in golf – he, an amateur, was going to win the Open Championship. Dr Purves was hurrying along at my elbow as we went, with the gallery, towards the sixteenth hole. 'Horace,' he said to me, in a voice of much solemnity, 'this is a great day for golf.' It was.
HORACE HUTCHINSON

Possibly Mr John Ball's driving, as a thing of artistic beauty, might be worthy of even higher praise if he did not reach down, in his own manner, with his right hand. But, taking it as it is, with all possible drawbacks, it commends itself to most golfers as the most perfect exhibition of the drive ever seen.
HORACE HUTCHINSON

Fewer strokes are thrown away by him on the putting green than by any other living player. He virtually never fails to lay the long putt dead, or hole the short one, and for the holing of the short putt he believes himself to have discovered a secret which he generously gives the world – you must keep the body absolutely still.
HORACE HUTCHINSON
of Harold Hilton

Willie Auchterlonie, Open Champion at the age of 21 in 1893, played relatively little competitive golf thereafter.

Instead, he set up a club-making business remarking: 'It's an awful empty life hitting golf balls every day; you are not giving much service.' These are not thoughts that would occur to many of today's tournament professionals.

MICHAEL HOBBS

In his day and in his own Scotland Freddie Tait was a national hero. I do not think I have ever seen any other golfer so adored by the crowd – no, not Harry Vardon nor Bobby Jones in their primes. It was a tremendous and to his adversaries an almost terrifying popularity. He was only 30 when he was killed; a brave young man, like many others who were killed; a thoroughly friendly creature, who made friends with all sorts and conditions of men, but not in any way possessed of an outstanding mind and character.

He was just a thoroughly good fellow who played a game very skilfully.

BERNARD DARWIN

He had a wonderfully gay and gallant way with him when playing a big match, a cheerful and brave and confident, though never a swaggering, way. Perhaps the crowd loved Freddie because he loved the crowd. He did not show by the movement of an eyebrow that he knew the crowd was there but he liked the tramp of feet behind him and the squeezing his way through the serried ranks around the putting green.

BERNARD DARWIN
of Freddie Tait

Most of all should I have liked to see Rolland on that occasion when he had come to play an exhibition match with Tom Dunn at Tooting Bec. The legend tells how Rolland had been tasting freely of the pleasures of the town and arrived at Tooting clad in his best clothes and a hard-boiled shirt front, and with no clubs. The shirt was crumpled into greater flexibility, some clubs were borrowed, and Rolland beat the record of the course and beat poor Tom Dunn into the middle of the ensuing week. There must have been something heroic and lovable about the man who could do that and in fact everybody adored Rolland; he had never an enemy but himself. I shall never quite get over the loss of not having seen him.

    BERNARD DARWIN

Someone has admirably described him in a championship as streaming ahead of the crowd like forked lightning and conveying the sense that thunderbolts are under his jurisdiction. His stocky and thickset body is impelled by a spirit that is for ever chafing to mount up like an eagle and his heart is occupied only by a titanic desire to get at somebody and flay him alive. There is indeed a murderous power about the man when he is really fighting for victory.

    HAROLD BEGBIE
    of J.H. Taylor

Give me a wind and I'll show you who'll be champion.

    BEN SAYERS

He is on the whole a very good putter though inclined in moments of stress to be short. How familiar is the picture of Sandy urging on his ball with frantic wavings of his putter on the last few inches of its course.

    BERNARD DARWIN
    of Sandy Herd

There is a special delight in seeing the kind of divine fury with which he laces into the ball, and yet the wonderful accuracy with which the club meets the ball.

    HORACE HUTCHINSON
    of James Braid

There are hitters who are reminiscent of howitzers in action, beneath whose feet the earth trembles; Braid seemed to impart the velocity of a bullet. It must have been a strain on the solid ball to have to pull itself together and refrain from bursting into pieces.

    H.N. WETHERED

We observed the bronzed face of Walter Hagen, together with the remaining players from the United States taking part in the Open Championship. On inquiring we were informed that the party were fulfilling a unanimous desire to pay homage and respect to the memory of Old Tom

Morris and his son, Young Tommy, who were buried in the cathedral grounds.

When the final appealing notes of 'The Last Post' had died away, Walter Hagen, who showed considerable emotion, took up his position at the head of the grave and all the golfers and their friends slowly filed past.

> D.M.M.

'Here Eddie, hold the flag while I putt out.'

> WALTER HAGEN
> to the Prince of Wales

When The Haig died in 1969, Junior called me from Detroit to tell me there would be no funeral. Instead, a bunch of his cronies were going to throw a party at the Detroit Athletic Club. They thought The Haig would prefer that.

I didn't go. Like Hamlet, golf's sweet prince, I thought, deserved a grander exit than that. He was splendid. They should have carried him out on a shield.

> CHARLES PRICE
> of Walter Hagen

I learned early that whatever I got out of life, I'd have to go out and get for myself. And the physical aptitude I possessed gave me the means of beginning. However, I had to create a paying market for that ability to play golf.

Showmanship was needed and happily I possessed a flair for that too and I used it. In fact, some fellows believed I invented the kind of showmanship which began to put golf on a big-time money basis. Apparently, too, it pleased the public to think I lived the easy carefree life, the playboy of golf. Frankly I was happy to support both those illusions, since I was making money out of the showmanship and I was having a grand time living on the money.

I was trying to make a living out of a game which had never in its history supplied more than the bare necessities to its professional players.

WALTER HAGEN
The Walter Hagen Story

That spurt was one for all the golfing ages. Whitcombe's spurt was as fine a one but there is a difference between the two, as there so often was between Hagen and the other man, that Hagen just won and the other man just didn't.

BERNARD DARWIN

Miss a putt for $2,000? Not likely!
WALTER HAGEN

Never hurry, never worry and always remember to smell the flowers along the way.

WALTER HAGEN

One has the impression of wide and irresistible shoulders acting like a great fly-wheel, revolving with such titanic force that if a golf ball had any volition of its own it would disappear into space without waiting to be crushed into submission.

H.N. WETHERED
on Cyril Tolley

The secret is a swing that gives no semblance of a chance of ever running out. Whether Mr Jones himself is conscious of all the microscopic divergences which he describes is a matter known only to himself. According to his own accounts he is always struggling; to the onlooker he is always triumphing. A shot is called for and the complementary swing is at once applied and the ball gracefully acquiesces. An imperative gesture is executed and the ball has no option but to comply.

    H.N. WETHERED

The 8th hole on Friday afternoon, with the breeze against, was a really long affair. Mr Jones hit a fine tee shot, and followed it with an almost equally fine brassie and lay within some 25 to 30 yards of the green. His third, which just reached the green, was worthy of a 10-handicap player not at his best; his fourth, very short, was worthy of an honest full-blooded rabbit; his fifth would not have got him a club handicap; and his sixth was reminiscent of an LGU 36. Mr Jones had taken a 7.

    E.M. COCKELL
    Bobby Jones still won the 1930 British Open

And now it was goodbye to golf. And I could still say what I had said to people all over the world. They could see for themselves if he was a golfer, but I could tell them that he was a much finer young man than he was a golfer. Wholly lacking in affectation, modest to the degree of shyness, generous and thoughtful of his opponents, it is not likely that his equal will come again.

So Bobby Jones, the greatest competitive athelete of history closed the book on the bright lexicon of championships, with every honour in the world to grace its final chapter.

The *New York Times* fittingly commented: 'With dignity he quit the memorable scene on which he nothing common did, or mean.'

It was the end of the trail for both of us. And the end was good.

    O.B. KEELER
    The Bobby Jones Story

I suspect that the Jones humour has been what really got him through all those trying years of being a celebrity in our country.

Well, what more can I say for my hero? He was a gentleman and there was laughter in his heart and on his lips, and he loved his friends.

PAUL GALLICO
Farewell to Sport

About three days before Jones's death, when he knew he was dying, he said to the members of his family, 'If this is all there is to it, it sure is peaceful.' That is good to know. We were lucky we had Jones so long, for he had a rare gift for passing ideas and ideals on to other people. I think he probably enriched more lives than anyone else I have known. He enriched mine beyond measure.

HERBERT WARREN WIND

Running through all his golf is that vein of pugnacity. Archie Compston is always prepared to meet anybody, anywhere, any time for any sum, and will walk on the first tee with an unbounded belief in his own ability to win.

E.M. COCKELL

If we all played golf like Mac Smith, the National Open Championship could be played on one course every day in the year and never a divot mark would scar the beautiful fairway. He treats the grass of a golf course as though it were an altar cloth.

TOMMY ARMOUR

A NATURAL ENQUIRY: "MUMMY, WHAT'S THAT MAN FOR?"

He dresses like a gardener and usually plays like one.

HENRY COTTON
of 1935 Open Champion Alf Perry

While some of his rivals have been content to go along in a somewhat lackadaisical manner, working on odd theories from time to time and practising when it suited them, he has been trying to discover the why and wherefore of every little movement that takes place during the swing. Some say it has caused him to waste too much of his energy on the unessentials of the game. It does not represent my view. I think that this passion for knowledge has been largely responsible for his success.

 HENRY LONGHURST
 on Henry Cotton

He came from nowhere and went back there.

 ANON.
 of 1935 Open Champion Alf Perry

I held the putter in a vice-like grip and from the moment I took it back from the ball I was blind and unconscious.

 TOMMY ARMOUR
 commenting on how he had holed the putt which
 won him the 1931 Open Championship

Tommy Armour is a great golfer – a superlative golfer. But he is something more than that – he is a personage. He has what it takes to stand out from the herd. There have been moments when I would have liked to shove an icicle through his cold heart; there have been moments when I wish his confounded Scottish consonants would split splinters off his front teeth; but for all that, at any time, I will take a long train ride to spend an evening with him. I guess I like him.

 CLARENCE BUDDINGTON KELLAND

Sam Snead was once told a very funny story about gambling at golf. He laughed so loud you could have heard a pin drop.

PORKY OLIVER

Actually, Ben didn't leave himself much time for laughter. I can't recall him ever finding humour in anything that happened on the golf course. Golf was his business – a tough business, full of disappointments.

FRED CORCORAN

I just try to put it on the fairway, then the green and not threeputt.

PETER THOMSON

Mr Bing Crosby, the singer, has been in Europe for the last three months dividing his time unequally between making radio tape recordings for America and playing golf. As far as Crosby is concerned, the radio broadcasts are something to do on a rainy day but his golf is not a joking matter and the crooner can be found on the St Cloud golf course almost every sunny day.

ART BUCHWALD
The *New York Herald Tribune*

How about that amigo. I just come over to see my friends and I win ze bloody championship.

ROBERTO DE VICENZO
on winning the 1967 Open Championship

Maybe you think I'm a stupid Argentine, but you spell my name wrong on the seating plan, the place cards and the menu – and different each time.

ROBERTO DE VINCENZO

at an official dinner after he had failed to tie for the 1968 Masters after signing an incorrect scorecard

Hagen said that no one remembers who finished second. But they still ask me if I ever think about that putt I missed to win the 1970 Open at St Andrews. I tell them that sometimes it doesn't cross my mind for a full five minutes.

DOUG SANDERS

There are many who have argued that success spoiled Tony Jacklin. Wealth poured down upon him and the lad from Scunthorpe was well satisfied, not having that so necessary desire to be the greatest golfer in the world. Yet we might remember that only the truly greatest stay long at the top. For seven or eight years Jacklin was there. Why should we demand more?

MICHAEL HOBBS

Real pressure in golf is playing for $10 when you've only got $5 in your pocket.

LEE TREVINO

We tournament golfers are much overrated. We get paid too much.

TOM WATSON

I had a reputation for being tough. You had to be when you were Italian.

GENE SARAZEN

I would rather play Hamlet with no rehearsal than TV golf.
    JACK LEMMON

You have the hands, now play with your heart.
    ROBERTO DE VICENZO
    to Seve Ballesteros before he won the 1979 Open
    Championship

They say I get in too many bunkers. But is no problem. I am
the best bunker player.
    SEVERIANO BALLESTEROS
    after winning the 1979 Open Championship

My swing is faultless.
    IAN WOOSNAM

Of all the golfers in the world I cannot believe that anyone will make a greater impact upon the championships than this very tough, very determined young man. The world is at his feet and he is only 21 years of age.

PAT WARD THOMAS
of Jack Nicklaus

I think I fail a bit less than everyone else.
JACK NICKLAUS

So how did Nicklaus win so much? Because he could finish a hole better than anyone else. As a player he's the greatest of all time but as a golfer I can't even put him in the first fifty.

WILD BILL MEHLHORN

Nicklaus plays a kind of golf with which I am not familiar.
BOBBY JONES

He is the most immeasurable of golf champions. But this is not entirely true because of all he has won, or because of that mysterious fury with which he has managed to rally himself. It is partly because of the nobility he has brought to losing. And more than anything because of the pure unmixed joy he has brought to trying.

DAN JENKINS
of Arnold Palmer

The answer to Hogan is, I fancy, that if Hogan means to win, you lose.

HENRY LONGHURST

I couldn't wait for the sun to come up the next morning so that I could get out on the course again.

BEN HOGAN

I try to work with God as a partner.
GARY PLAYER

Why that would be like me challenging Bing Crosby to a singing contest, wouldn't it?
BEN HOGAN
on hearing of a challenge from the reigning British Open champion

Arnold Palmer is an early riser. He is anxious to get the day going because who knows how many good things might happen.
MARK MCCORMACK

I'm almost delighted I lost. I might have turned pro otherwise.
BILLY JOE PATTON

One of the remarkable things about Walter Hagen was the fact that, even in their defeat, his opponents all had tremendous affection for him.
FRED CORCORAN

Ben Hogan will keep winning championships as long as he wants to badly enough.

BOBBY JONES

There is no other loser in sport who has shown himself to be as gracious and warm as Nicklaus has shown himself to be.

HERBERT WARREN WIND

Seve Ballesteros is a rare kind of guy. He's an excitable golfer who can still concentrate.

LARRY NELSON

In those days [the 1930s] the money was the main thing, the *only* thing I played for. Championships were something to grow old with.

BYRON NELSON

If I had to have someone putt a 20-footer for everything I own – my house, my cars, my family – I'd want Nicklaus to putt it for me.

DAVE HILL

The King's guards shall attend him at the church and also when he goeth to the fields to walk or goff.

LORD LOTHIAN
referring to Charles II

Hell, it ain't like losing a leg!

BILLY JOE PATTON
after losing the Masters

So, in the summer of 1968, a young golfer from Texas experienced something that would forever change his life. Not only did I fall in love with formal tournament competition, but I was enraptured with so many other facets of the game: the different courses, the people, the history and traditions.

BEN CRENSHAW

If Charles II felt in any way troubled he was at least allowed to have recourse to the distractions of golf.

SAMUEL R. GARDINER, 1894

I have always thought that Young Tom Morris was the greatest golfer that ever lived; today, I believe that Bobby Jones is equally wonderful. He is the reincarnation of Young Tom. I have known both more or less intimately and I am familiar with the conditions under which each played: Young Tom on an unkempt, rough course with the gutta ball, Bobby on a smooth, parklike perfectly kept course with the rubber-cored ball. To my mind, these two are the greatest golfers in history, both as to execution, clean sportsmanship, courtesy, equable temperament, and most attractive personality.

CHARLES BLAIR MACDONALD, 1928

From his amiable temperament and obliging disposition, his gentlemanly appearance and manly bearing, combined with that undaunted determination which so marked his play, Young Tom became a great favourite with everyone with whom he played; and these lines cannot better be concluded than with the remark of one, writing since his death, who played often with him, and was a good judge of the game – 'Tommy,' says he, 'was the best player who ever addressed himself to a ball.'

ANON., 1876

The ugly specter of racism in golf reared its head in America as early as 1896. In the second US Open, held that year at Shinnecock Hills, a group of professionals threatened to boycott play if John Shippen, of black and Indian parentage, was allowed to compete. The first USGA president, Theodore Havemeyer, refused to bar him.

    BUD DUFNER

I guess about 15 yards.

    GARY PLAYER

    in response to a question as to how much extra length his fitness routines had given him.

King Charles I is said to have been fond of the exercise of the golf. While he was engaged in a party of golf on the Links of Leith, a letter was delivered into his hands, which gave him the first account of the rebellion in Ireland.

    WILLIAM TYTLER, 1792

The King [Charles I] was nowhere treated with more honour than at Newcastle, both he and his train having liberty to go abroad and play at Goff in the Shield Field, without the walls.

    JOHN SYKES, 1833

A big-name winner like Palmer is a modern King Midas. Everything he drinks, smokes, wears or drives can turn to gold. All he has to do is testify, yes, that's what I put on my hair, smoke, drink, wear, drive, swing and hit.

    TONY LEMA

Walter arrived late.

'I was shaving,' he explained easily.

'Shaving?' I asked. 'You must have had a month-old beard to get rid of.'

Hagen shook his head and smiled. 'No,' he said, 'You see, when I have a match to play I begin to relax as soon as I wake up. Everything I do, I do slow and easy. That goes for stroking the razor, getting dressed, and eating my breakfast. I'm practically in slow motion. By the time I'm ready to tee off, I'm so used to taking my time that it's impossible to hurry my swing.'

JOHNNY FARRELL

After a golfer has been out on the circuit for a while he learns how to handle his dating so that it doesn't interfere with his golf. The first rule usually is no woman-chasing after Wednesday.

TONY LEMA

When I stepped forward to take his bag, which was almost as big and heavy as I was, he raised his eyes in surprise. But before he could say what I knew he was thinking – that I was too small – I spoke up.

'That's all right Mr Hagen, I am the best caddie in Brisbane.'

Hagen looked down at me. 'OK son, then you and I are a pair, because I am the best golfer in Brisbane.'

NORMAN VON NIDA

The putter which Locke uses has often been called his magic wand. It was given him in 1926 and was a long wooden shafted rusty old club with a small upright iron blade. Locke treasures it above all his possessions and on his first visit to the United States he was so fearful of losing it that he slept with it at night.

RONALD NORVAL

A match against Bobby Jones is just as though you got your hand caught in a buzz saw. He coasts along serenely waiting for you to miss a shot, and the moment you do he has you on the hook and you never get off. He can drive straighter than any man living. He is perfectly machine-like in his iron play, and on the greens he is a demon.

FRANCIS OUIMET

Harry Vardon stands alone in all the glory that his performances testify.

J.H. TAYLOR

Little did I guess when playing him [Harry Vardon] at Ganton that I was playing a man who was to make golfing history and develop into – what is my solemn and considered judgement – the finest and most finished golfer that the game has ever produced. I have seen and watched every player of eminence during the past fifty years and taking into account everything they have done I still hold that my opinion is sound, and I am willing to uphold it even if the world should be against me.

J.H. TAYLOR

If I wanted to know how I had played, I awaited the next day's account in *The Times*. With what was therein written I was content, for here was the truth of things. I want nothing more than to be remembered by posterity in the words of Bernard Darwin.

J.H. TAYLOR

21 January I thought upon the way of playeing at golve. I found that the first point to be studied in playeing at the golve is to hitt the ball exactly; for if you hitt the ball exactly though the club have butt strenth yett the ball will fly verie farre. The way to attain this perfection is to play with little strenth at first but yet acuratly observing all the rules of poustaur and motion and then when ye have acquired ane habit of hitting the ball exactly ye most learn to incresse your strenth to force in the stroak by degrees, staying still so long upon every degree till you have acquired ane habit of it; neither will the knowledge of these degrees be altogether uselese afterward, for they will serve for halfe chops, and quarter chops, and for holling the ball.

THOMAS KINCAID, 1687

I have been consulting Ben Hogan's book, *Power Golf*, to see whether, unlike so many golfers who write books, he practises what he preaches. The answer is 'Yes, he does'. I never saw anything quite like it. By taking his club far away from him on the backswing, and then almost as far back round his neck as our own James Adams, and then thrusting it even further away in front after impact he attains the swing of at least a six-footer. His right arm never bends after impact and it finishes in a position with which the middle-aged reader may care at his own risk to experiment, namely dead straight and pointing, almost horizontally, behind his head. 'The speed and momentum,' says the caption, 'have carried me to a full finish.' They would carry most of us to the infirmary.

    HENRY LONGHURST

In no game is the player provided with such a staggering wealth of instruction. There is hardly one stroke in golf which a man cannot play at least a dozen different ways, yet remain, according to the information of the masters, correct in method. This state of affairs is almost horrifying. It occurs in no other pastime.

    R.C. ROBERTSON-GLASGOW

The majority treat the hole as a place more difficult to get into than it really is. Now the fact is, that (from short distances) the hole is pretty big, and from all distances is capable of catching a ball going at a fair pace. Many more putts would go in if players credited holes with a little of that catching power which they really possess.

    SIR WALTER SIMPSON
    The Art of Golf

To the beginner putting seems the least interesting part of the game. Like other things, essentially foolish in themselves, such as preaching, putting becomes attractive in proportion to the skill acquired in it.

    SIR WALTER SIMPSON
    The Art of Golf

A good drive enables you to play the rest of the hole.

    ANON.

Let the club swing itself through. Help it on all you can but do not you begin to hit with it. Let it do its work itself and it will do it well. Interfere with it, and it will be quite adequately revenged.

    HORACE HUTCHINSON
    Golf

Every beginner ought to play with better golfers than himself. He will unconsciously by that means aim higher. It should be his ambition to beat somebody, and, having done so, to attack a still stronger adversary.

    SIR WALTER SIMPSON
    The Art of Golf

Just knock hell out of it with your right hand.
    TOMMY ARMOUR

Sometimes he thinks it's all in the hands, and then in the shoulders, and even in the knees. When it's in the knees he can't control it. Basketball was somehow more instinctive. If you thought about merely walking down the street the way you think about golf you'd wind up falling off the curb. Yet a good straight drive or a soft chip stiff to the pin gives him the bliss that used to come thinking of women, imagining if only you and she were alone on some island.

 JOHN UPDIKE

Oh hang it! With so many things to be thought of all at once, steady play is impossible.

 SIR WALTER SIMPSON

Give me a man with big hands and big feet and no brains and I'll make a golfer out of him.

 WALTER HAGEN

Only one golfer in a thousand grips the club lightly enough.

 JOHNNY MILLER

If I didn't know my distances to a yard, I couldn't break 80 on any golf course.

 LEE TREVINO

When I want a long ball, I spin my hips faster.

 JACK NICKLAUS

Golf is a hands game.

 HENRY COTTON

All good players have good hands. And I'm afraid you have to be born with them.

 DAVE STOCKTON

Golf is played with the arms.
SAM SNEAD

You can talk to a fade but a hook won't listen.
LEE TREVINO

A leading difficulty with the average player is that he totally misunderstands what is meant by concentration. He may think he is concentrating hard when he is merely worrying.
R.T. JONES

Every good golfer keeps his left hand leading the clubhead through impact.
LEE TREVINO

Power in golf has become totally out of proportion. This is a game of precision, not strength, and that aspect has become so important to me that I plan my playing programme accordingly. I just do not want to play those long, dull, wide-open turf nursery courses any more. Where is the challenge in just beating at the ball? Length is only one factor. Golf should make you think, and use your eyes, your intelligence and your imagination. Variety and precision are more important than power and length.

JACK NICKLAUS

Through the ball we are all the same. We just have different ways of getting it there.

CHARLES COODY

Carrying clubs is one of the most agreeable trades open to the lower orders. In it an amount of drunkenness is tolerated which in any other would land the men in the workhouse. A very low standard of efficiency and very little work will secure a man a decent livelihood. If he is civil, willing to carry for three or four hours a day, and not apt to drink to excess before his work is done, he will earn a fair wage, and yet be able to lie abed till nine in the morning like a lord. A caddy may rise to be a green-keeper or a club-master, and after his death be better known to fame than many a defunct statesman or orator.

SIR WALTER SIMPSON
The Art of Golf

Caddie (after the local vicar had removed a vast divot with a wild swing): 'Shall I replace it sir, or would you like to keep it for the harvest festival?'

Caddie (infuriated by his advice being ignored gives the player the wrong line, the ball finishing in a clump of gorse): 'If you are so clever sir, let's see you get out of that.'

MICHAEL HOBBS

'The caddies will only drink the more if overpaid,' you say.
Indeed! and to what good purpose do you apply the money
you grudge to the poor? Is there something nobler in your
gout and dyspepsia than in my caddie's red nose?

SIR WALTER SIMPSON

From men who have adopted carrying as a trade, the golfer
is entitled to expect the highest standard of efficiency. If he
carries for you regularly, he ought to know what club you
intend to take, and to give it without being asked. When

you are in doubt about how to play your shot, he ought to confirm you in the opinion you have formed regarding it. He must never show the just contempt he has for your game.

SIR WALTER SIMPSON
The Art of Golf

I was lying 10th and had a 35-foot putt. I whispered over my shoulder: 'How does this one break?' And my caddy said 'Who cares?'

JACK LEMMON

The only time I talk on a golf course is to my caddie. And then only to complain when he gives me the wrong club.

SEVERIANO BALLESTEROS

The grounds on which golf is played are called links, being the barren sandy soil from which the sea has retired in recent geological times. In their natural state links are covered with long, rank bent grass and gorse.

Links are too barren for cultivation: but sheep, rabbits, geese and professionals pick up a precarious livelihood on them.

SIR WALTER SIMPSON

A golf course is a field of manoeuvre and action, employing the military and engineering side of the game. It opens up a series of tactical and strategical opportunities, the implications of which it would be well for every golfer to grasp. It is important to emphasise the necessity for the golfer to use his head as much as his hands; or to make his mental agility match his physical ability.

H.N. WETHERED and TOM SIMPSON
The Architectural Side of Golf

Undulation is the soul of golf.
     H.N. WETHERED

A golf course may be said to have to satisfy four definite requirements. It must supply the opportunity for the pleasure of practising an athletic art, entail the necessity of providing an adequate test of skill, demand mental agility, and, lastly, a disciplinary scheme by which the virtuous cannot be rewarded without a penalty being inflicted on the sinner.
     PETER LAWLESS

We will take the average length of a good drive to be 170 yards. 170 yards then is a good length for a hole. So is 340 yards, and so is 510. In each of these cases the man who hits his one, two or three shots well has his reward. But what a vast number of links do we find laid out in utter disregard of this essential principle. What a lot of holes do we find of that feeblest length of all – somewhere between two and three hundred so that he who has hit a rasper from the tee is scarcely better off than he who has topped.
     HORACE HUTCHINSON, 1890

If a man is to get into a hazard let it be a bad one. Let the lies within your hazard be as bad as you please – the worse the better. So leave your whins without any pruning or thinning and if the bottom of your sand bunker gets smooth-beaten, howk it up.
     HORACE HUTCHINSON, 1890

Macdonald loved his course so much that his private home was not placed to take advantage of the best possible views but was faced, instead, to look down on his golf links. He ran his club with an iron hand. He was famous for listening to criticisms, rectifying them, and then sending the bill to whoever had complained.

GEORGE PLIMPTON
The Bogey Man

Ladies' links should be laid out on the model, though on a smaller scale, of the 'long round'; containing some short putting holes, some longer holes, admitting of a drive or two of 70 or 80 yards, and a few suitable hazards. We venture to suggest 70 or 80 yards as the average limit of a drive advisedly; not because we doubt a lady's power to make a longer drive, but because that cannot well be done without raising the club above the shoulder. The posture and gestures requisite for a full swing are not particularly graceful when the player is clad in female dress.

LORD WELLWOOD
Golf

These greens are so fast I have to hold my putter over the ball and hit it with the shadow.

SAM SNEAD

The fairways were so narrow you had to walk down them single file.

SAM SNEAD

From what has been said as to the changes in the links, the balls, and the clubs, it is obvious that the round ought to be done in much fewer strokes now than formerly. How many fewer it is not easy accurately to determine. Some say 20. I incline to think 15 or 16, but I believe that every year it will be done in fewer for some little time, as the course gets broader and the hazards fewer.

JAMES BALFOUR, 1887
of St Andrews

St Andrews is drenched in golf. It reminds me of a Spanish town when bull-fighting is afoot. Every man, woman, and child seems to have a stake in the game. The butcher, the baker, and the candlestick-maker but finish their day's work to be off to the links.

PETER LAWLESS

Crosse at Chantilly

Until you play it, St Andrews looks like the sort of real estate you couldn't give away.

SAM SNEAD

Even in defeat, the scenic surroundings at Pebble Beach were absolutely dazzling, the dream of an artist who had been drinking gin and sobering up on absinthe. It is too extravagantly decorated not to be a painting. Snow-white sand in the bunkers; vividly green turf, coccusbent green. The Bay of Naples is no more lovely and not as blue as the inlet, Carmel Bay, along which the course is built.

O.B. KEELER
The Bobby Jones Story

Folks praise the links ayont the Forth –
St Andrews, Elie, Leven:
About Carnoustie, Dornoch Firth,
Our ears they aft are deavin'.

But Gullane, oh, your wondrous charm
A' other links surpasses;
Inspired we climb your links as once
The ancients climbed Parnassus.

ANON.

There is a sense of privilege as well as rare experience in visiting Pine Valley, for it has no parallel anywhere. No course presents more vividly and more severely the basic challenge of golf – the balance between fear and courage. Nowhere is the brave and beautiful shot rewarded so splendidly in comparison to the weak and faltering; nowhere is there such a terrible contrast between reward and punishment, and yet the examination is just.

PAT WARD THOMAS
The Manchester Guardian

Of the four hundred odd courses on which I have played, including some on which no blade of grass had ever grown or ever will, El Fasher remains unique. There was no

clubhouse and no tees, but there were nine greens, each
with a hole in, generally with the metal rim sticking up out
of the sand, so that a local rule said: 'On the rim counts in.'
We teed off in the sand at the top of a bluff looking over a
magnificent view and played down to the 1st hole, marked
by a small boy in a nightshirt holding what turned out to be
the club's only flag. No use having permanent flags, they
said. If you had wooden ones, the ants would eat them and,
if you had metal, the locals would melt them instantly
down for spears.

> HENRY LONGHURST
> *My Life and Soft Times*

The finishes of the Masters Tournament have almost always
been dramatic and exciting. It is my conviction that this
has been because of the make-or-break quality of the
second nine. This nine, with its abundant water hazards,
each creating a perilous situation, can provide excruciating
torture for the front runner trying to hang on. Yet it can
yield a very low score to the player making a closing rush. It
has been played in thirty during the tournament and in the
medium forties by players still in the running at the time.

> R.T. JONES
> *Golf is My Game*

At Westward Ho! we step straight into the pure air of
sanctity, an open plain and limitless sky; and if we are
capable of an emotion worthy of the occasion we shall hear
the sound of an invisible and celestial choir echoing in our
ears. One lives and plays there for a while amongst the
gods. Golf becomes a symbolic and religious act.

> H.N. WETHERED and TOM SIMPSON

When a tourist drives through Switzerland, he is staggered by its prodigal beauty; around the corner from the most wondrous view he has ever beheld he comes upon a view that surpasses it – and on and on, endlessly. Ballybunion is something like that. One stirring hole is followed by another and another.

> HERBERT WARREN WIND
> *The New Yorker*

The trick for the developer, as devised through his architect, is to build something that is photogenically stunning, however impractical, extravagant or absurd. Never mind the golfer, that most gullible of all citizens.

> PETER THOMSON

I try to build courses for the most enjoyment by the greatest number.

> ALISTER MACKENZIE

The mystique of Muirfield lingers on. So does the memory of Carnoustie's foreboding. So does the scenic wonder of Turnberry, and the haunting incredibility of Prestwick, and the pleasant deception of Troon. But put them all together and St Andrews can play their low ball for atmosphere.

> DAN JENKINS

St Andrews never impressed me at all. I wondered how it got such a reputation. The only reason could be on account of its age.

> BILL MEHLHORN

After the Restoration, James Duke of York was sent to Edinburgh, and his favourite pastimes appear to have been the torturing of the adherents to the Covenant, and the playing of golf on the Links of Leith.

> JOHN ROBERTSON

Dyvers inhabitants of the burgh repairs upon the Sabboth day to the town of Leith, and in tyme of sermons are sene vagrant about the streets, drynking in taverns, or otherwayes at golf, aicherie, or other pastymes, uponn the linkes, thairby profaning the Sabboth day.

EDINBURGH COUNCIL, 1593

About this toun are the fairest and largest linkes of any pairt of Scotland, fitt for Archery, Goffing, Ryding, and all other exercises; they doe surpasse the feilds of Montrose or St Andrews.

SIR ROBERT GORDON
writing about Dornoch, 1630

A good golf course is like good music. It does not necessarily appeal the first time one plays it.
ALISTER MACKENZIE

'The man who hates golfers' is what they call me. They couldn't be more wrong. I design holes that are fun to play.
ROBERT TRENT JONES

The reason the Road hole at St Andrews is the most difficult par 4 in the world is that it was designed as a par 6.
BEN CRENSHAW

St Andrews? I feel like I'm back visiting an old grandmother. She's crotchety and eccentric but also elegant. Anyone who doesn't fall in love with her has no imagination.
TONY LEMA

By all means screw their women and drink their booze but never write one word about their bloody awful golf courses.
HENRY LONGHURST
advice to a fellow journalist being pressed to make a trip to a new expensive golf development.

That Wentworth is a sonofabitch.
SAM SNEAD

Forget Cypress Point and the others. This is easily the finest course in the world, the absolute number one. I am glad it is difficult to get here and I am not going to tell anyone about Dornoch. I want to keep it for myself, the way it is, and come back every year until I die.
AMERICAN GOLF ARCHITECT

I'm glad I brought this course, this monster, to its knees.
BEN HOGAN

You would like to gather up several holes from Prestwick and mail them to your top ten enemies.
DAN JENKINS

Courses built for 300 yard tee shot artists are not great courses.
PETER THOMSON

At Jinja there is both hotel and golf course. The latter is, I believe, the only course in the world which posts a special rule that the player may remove his ball from hippopotamus footprints.
EVELYN WAUGH

Golf architects can't play golf themselves and make damn sure that no one else can.
ANON.

Forty years ago, and indeed from time immemorial, the only kind of ball with which golf had been played was made of leather stuffed with feathers till it was as hard as gutta-percha.
A man could make only four balls in a day. These balls did not last long, perhaps not more than one round. They opened at the seams, especially in wet weather.
JAMES BALFOUR, 1887

Had the gutta-percha golf ball not been invented, it is likely enough that golf itself would now be in the catalogue of virtually extinct games, only locally surviving, as stool-ball and knurr and spell.

HORACE HUTCHINSON, 1899

Hail, Gutta-Percha! precious gum!
O'er Scotland's links lang may ye bum;
Some proud-pursed billies haw and hum,
And say ye'er douf at fleein';
But let them try ye fairly out,
Wi' ony balls for days about,
Your merits they will loudly tout,
And own they hae been leein'.

WILLIAM GRAHAM, 1848

The advent of the rubber ball was instrumental in creating an entirely different method of striking the object. The solid ball required to be hit for carry, whereas it was quickly apparent that the Haskell lent itself to an enormous run. I hold the firm opinion that from this date the essential attitude towards accuracy was completely lost sight of. This was the start of the craze for length and still more length.

HARRY VARDON, 1933

To control his own ball, all alone without help or hindrance, the golfer must first and last control himself. At each stroke, the ball becomes a vital extension, an image of one's innermost self.

JOHN STUART MARTIN
The Curious History of the Golf Ball

What a farce is this business of length! Golf is surely the only game, either in the United States or Britain, whose whole character has been changed solely by so-called 'improvements' in the instruments with which it is played. None of these changes have been solicited by, or had the approval of, the ruling body. Year by year we have altered 36,000 tees, and the Americans, I suppose, have altered 90,000, to accommodate Messrs –'s confounded new ball. Year by year we walk farther and farther and year by year get fewer shots in the process.

I cannot believe that the parties concerned would alter the stands at Wimbledon, Forest Hills, Wembley and the Yankee Stadium simply to accommodate a new ball, which, when struck in the same manner, happened to go further. I rather fancy they would tell the manufacturers what to do with their new ball.

HENRY LONGHURST
Round in Sixty-Eight

83

The niblick, with its heavy head of iron, is a capital club for knocking down solicitors.
     ANON.

John Ball was using the Haskell ball and doing such wonders with it that I found myself envying him. I had not seen the rubber-cored ball before and when we reached the 15th hole, Mr Ball, smiling at my comments regarding his drives, gave me a Haskell to try. That was the end of the gutty ball for me.
     SANDY HERD

I found very little difference in the length of drive between the Haskell and gutta balls; perhaps they run further, but certainly don't carry as far. They are also more difficult to stop when approaching and on the putting green are very liable to jump out of the hole.
     JAMES BRAID

I really do not see why we should allow the Haskell to come in. It should be slaughtered at the ports. The discovery of a ball that flies considerably further would be a menace to the game of golf. It would immediately make all our holes the wrong length.
     Manchester Guardian, 1901

No power on earth will deter men from using a ball that will add to the length of their drive.
     Golf Illustrated, 1902

One never realised what a stubborn, inert thing a gutty is until the Haskell came on the scene.
     Golf Illustrated, 1902

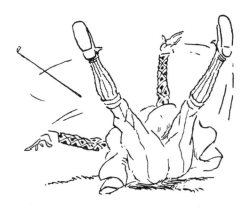

There's no muckle wrong wi' the Haskell.
ANDREW KIRKALDY

Here one makes clubs fine and noble.
Play colf with pleasure, not brawls.
Play for a pint or a gallon.
Let the winter be cold and hard,
We play the ball just the same.
HOUSE SIGN IN HAARLEM, 1650

Ye will remember to bring with you ane dossen of commoun golf ballis to me and David Moncrieff.
LETTER FROM THE ORKNEYS, 1585

The golfer ties his ice spurs on,
Or finds something rough to stand on
For skiddy ice, if snowless
Laughs and jests at smooth soles.
    ANON.
    Holland, 1657

I laid out the balls in a line, had a waggle with the wedge, felt all right, so I shaped up to the first ball, began the old slow motion backswing and suddenly everything went mad. I thought I wasn't going to hit it at all. The club was too short. The ball too small. I took a quick little lurch and caught it with the very edge of the sole. The ball took off as though struck by a full 2-iron, a foot above the ground and going like a bullet. It snored between two olive trees and disappeared through the cypress hedge. A split second later there was a tremendous metallic crash. I had struck either the front or the rear door of a large white car, which had been passing slowly down the road.

It stopped. Four people – elderly I thought – got out. Two men and two women. I heard the beginning of querulous questions.

'What is it that it is?'

'But what, M'sieu Thierry, has passed itself?'

Then fear – and fury – started to take over.

'One has shot at us!'

'Some imbecile has discharged his fowling piece.'

'We will carry plaint to the police – to the town hall!'

'One must search for the assassin –'

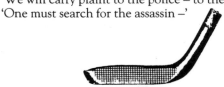

PUTTER.

The assassin stood very still, very thin and upright, squeezing himself into the shape of a ruler behind the sheltering trunk of an olive tree.

    PATRICK CAMPBELL
    Patrick Campbell's Golfing Book

'Who is the best lefthand player you ever saw,' said Mr Bliss, himself a lefthander and playing the game of his life.

    'Never saw one that was worth a damn,' Harry Vardon replied.

    MICHAEL HOBBS

For the 1920 US Open, the future superstar, Bobby Jones, playing his first Open, was paired with the great Harry Vardon, then the greatest player the game had seen.

Early in the round, Jones thinned a simple short pitch right through a green.

Red with embarrassment he turned to Vardon and said: 'Mr Vardon, have you ever seen a worse shot than that!'

'No,' Vardon replied.

    MICHAEL HOBBS

I was playing golf the other day
That the Germans landed;
All our troops had run away,
All our ships were stranded;
And the thought of England's shame
Altogether spoilt my game.
    ANON.

Hush-a-bye, baby, pretty one, sleep;
Daddy's gone golfing to win the club sweep.
If he plays nicely (I hope that he will)
Mother will show him her dressmaker's bill

Hush-a-bye, baby, safe in your cot;
Daddy's come home, and his temper is hot.
Cuddle down closer, baby of mine;
Daddy went round in a hundred and nine!
    ANON.

G. Odoreida, I am glad to say, did not often play golf. By his sheer ruthlessness, of course, Odoreida could shock the most hardened gamesman. Woe to the man who asked him as a guest to his golf club.

He would start with some appalling and unexpected thrust. He would arrive perhaps in a motor propelled invalid chair. Why? Or his hair would be cropped so close to the head that he seemed almost bald.

Worse still he would approach some average player of dignified and gentlemanly aspect and, for no reason, *ask for his autograph*. Again, why? One was on tenterhooks, always.

STEPHEN POTTER

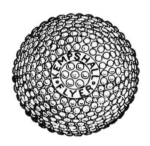

I don't trust doctors. They are like golfers. Every one has a different answer to your problem.

SEVERIANO BALLESTEROS

My luck is so bad that if I bought a cemetery people would stop dying.

ED FURGOL

Golf and sex are the only things you can enjoy without being good at them.

JIMMY DEMARET

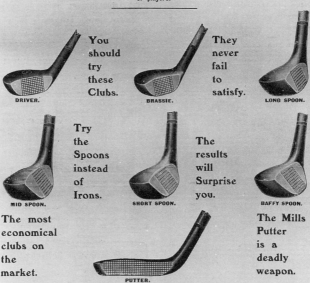

When I dine with Mr Snead he always suggests that I order as if I was expecting to pay for it myself. I have known many great destroyers of money, but Mr Snead is not among them.

GEORGE LOW

One afternoon a member came into my office and said: 'There's a fellow with a big Alsatian dog on the 9th. I've chased him off.' That trespasser was a police dog handler we had invited to train his dog and keep vandals off it.

GOLF CLUB SECRETARY

In the USA a number of first class golfers take as long to choose a wife as a club. Sometimes they make the wrong choice in each case.

DAI REES

Look like a woman but play like a man.

JAN STEPHENSON

Twice Open Champion Willie Park coined the slogan: 'The man who can putt is a match for anyone.' To which J.H. Taylor produced the response: 'The man who can approach does not need to putt.'
MICHAEL HOBBS

It's good sportsmanship not to pick up lost balls while they are still rolling.
MARK TWAIN

Is my friend in the bunker or is the bastard on the green?
ANON.

DRIVING.

There is only one way to travel to golf, believe me, and that is first class at the expense of Lord Beaverbrook.
HENRY LONGHURST